OPTIONS TRADING CRASH COURSE

The Complete Guide From Beginners to Hero Using Trading Option. Step by Step to Make Money With Swing Trading & Day Trading Strategies and More

PARKER JASON STEVEN

© **Copyright 2021 - All rights reserved.**

The content contained within this book may not be reproduced, duplicated, or transmitted without direct written permission from the author or the publisher.

Under no circumstances will any blame or legal responsibility be held against the publisher, or author, for any damages, reparation, or monetary loss due to the information contained within this book, either directly or indirectly.

Table Of Contents

Introduction 8

Chapter 1

What is an Option? 10
  Taking the Risk 10
  Understanding Options 12
    Why Are Options Used? 12
    How Do Options Work? 13
    Some Key Terms That You Should Know About 14
  Why is Options Trading Worth the Risk? 15
    Advantages 16
    Disadvantages 17
  Styles of Options 18

Chapter 2

Getting Started With Options Trading 19
  Types of Options 20
    Call Option 20
    Put Option 22
    Exchange-Traded Option 23
    Over the Counter Options or OTC 24
    Options Based on Underlying Securities 25
    Options Based on Their Expiration Cycle 26

Employee Stock Options 27
Cash-Settled Options 28
Exotic Options...28
Intrinsic Value and Time Value of Options............ 29
    Intrinsic Value 30
    Time Value..30
    Why Do These Values Matter?.......................................31
Buying/Selling Call Options..................................... 32
Buying/Selling Put Options 37
Call Spreads... 39
    Bull Call Spread...39
    Bear Call Spread..41
The Long Straddle 43
The Long Strangle 45
Technical Analysis.. 47
    Support and Resistance Levels 48
    RSI or Relative Strength Index.......................................49
    Bollinger Bands 50
    IMI or Intraday Momentum Index................................51

Chapter 3

The Greeks 52
    Delta.. 53
    Gamma 54
    Theta 55
    Vega... 56
    Rho 58

Minor Greeks 58

Chapter 4

Swing Trading with Options 60
   What is Swing Trading? 61
   Support and Resistance Secrets 62
   Difference Between Trend Trader and Swing Trader
   63
   Going Long on a Stock 65
   How to Spot a Reversal Trend? 66
   How to Short a Stock With Options? 68
   Understanding a Candlestick Chart 70
      Hammer 72
      Inverse Hammer 72
      Bullish Engulfing 73
      Morning Star 73
      Piercing Line 73
      Three White Soldiers 74
      Hanging Man 74
      Shooting Star 75
      Evening Star 75
      Bearish Engulfing 76
      Three Black Crows 76

Chapter 5

Iron Condor 77
   What is the Iron Condor? 77
   Understanding the Iron Condor 78

Profits and Losses 80
Iron Condor Example 81

Chapter 6

Bearish Strategies **83**
    Long Put 84
    Short Call 85
    Put Ratio Strategy 87
    Bear Call Strategy 88
    Bear Put Strategy 90
    Bear Put Ladder Spread 91

Chapter 7

The Option Trader's Mindset – 10 Traits That
Should be Present **93**
    Manage Risk Successfully 94
    Don't Make Mistake With Numbers 95
    Practice Discipline 96
    Don't Rush 97
    Figure Out Your Trading Style 100
    Understand the News 103
    Always Be Eager to Learn More 104
    Be Flexible 106
    Always Have a Trading Plan 108
    Maintain Records 113

Chapter 8

How to Maximize Profits? **116**

What Are the Challenges That You Will Face in Options Trading?... 117
Make Use of Trailing Stops.. 118
Practice Booking Profit Partially at Targets.......... 120
When to Take Profits in a Trade? 121

Chapter 9

Risk Management Techniques............................... **125**
Determine Risk/Exposure Upfront 126
Set Optimal Stop Loss Level................................... 128
Diversify Your Portfolio... 130
    Diversify by Position Size 131
    Diversify by Trading Strategy 133
    Diversify by Strike Price...134
    Diversify by Time 135
Keep Your Risk Consistent and Manage Your Emotions... 136
Maintain a Positive Risk-Reward Ratio 138
Make the Best Use of Option Spreads 140

Conclusion... **141**

Introduction

Thank you for purchasing *Options Trading Crash Course*, and I hope that you get the answers that you are looking for.

Do you want to know how you can achieve success in the world of options trading? Well, then you are at the right place. In this book, I will teach you how to learn the ropes and yet not get intimidated by all those new strategies and rules. It's time you take a back seat and make your money work for you. Well, you are not exactly going to sit through the process because you have to strategize the entire thing. But there are many ways to go about it, and the beauty of options trading is that no matter what the market condition is, you can always play it to your advantage. Out of the endless strategies that are there, you will have to narrow down to those that you are comfortable with and that works for you.

But taking the first step is the most important part of all. With options, you have plenty of chances to minimize your risk, and moreover, it is completely in your hands as to how much risk you are willing to take in a trade. By the time you finish reading this book, I hope you will have a comprehensive idea of how options trading is done and how you can use it to fulfill your financial goals.

I have tried to make this book as comprehensive as possible. Please enjoy!

Chapter 1

What is an Option?

Before you start with trading, there are some things you need to know. These things will form your foundation, and once your foundation is strong, you can deal with anything that comes your way. In this chapter, we are going to learn some introductory things about options trading. If you want to start investing, there are numerous doors open in front of you, and there are multiple ways to fulfill your financial goals. But among all the tools of investment, one of the most crucial ones is options. Their main plus point is that they are very versatile, and compared to stocks; they are much more dynamic.

Taking the Risk

There are many securities in the world of investing where you can put your money and allow it to grow, for example, commodities, bonds, futures, stocks, mutual funds, options, and so on. Investors who are new to the stock market usually go for mutual funds. Do you know why? Because you do not have to actively manage anything – for a small amount, everything will be managed, and you need not worry at all. People who are here for larger gains often choose bonds and stock, and then there are those who invest in options. If you can learn and do it right, options can give you handsome returns as well.

But before that, what are options? They are contracts with the help of which you get the right to either sell or purchase any security. But keep in mind that you are under the obligation to do so; an options contract simply gives you the right. Options were originally invested as tools that will help you in risk management. In simpler terms, they were brought into this world so that a shift in the risk can be made from those who are risk-averse to those who want to take the risk. And thus, most beginners see options in the light of a risk-reducing entity, and thus, they somewhat end up gambling with their money.

How you use options in the world of investing is entirely in your hands. But I want to make sure that you understand that hedging risk and speculating risk are two entirely different concepts. Now coming to your question, do options contain risk? Well, the answer would depend on the type of trading you want to do. Not every option has the same level of risk. If you are an options buyer, then your risk would not match that of an options seller. We will discuss these things in detail as we move forward in the book. But the main point to keep in mind is that even if you are trading options, you should never put yourself in a position where you end up taking an unlimited risk.

Understanding Options

In this section, we are going to discuss some key concepts in the world of options trading that you should be aware of.

Why Are Options Used?
There are two main reasons why options are used, and they are

- **Speculation** – When you make a wager on the direction of price in the future, that is known as speculation. The speculator might perform technical or fundamental analysis and then speculate the price to go up in the near future. In that case, the speculator will purchase a call option on the stock. This will give them considerable leverage compared to buying the stock outright.

- **Hedging** – As I told you before, it was mainly because of hedging that options came into existence in the first place. The benefit is that at a reasonable price, you will be able to reduce the risk with the help of options. You can even say that options become your insurance policy. Just like you use an insurance policy to secure your health or your car, you are using options to secure the investments you have already made against a downturn.

How Do Options Work?

Options are mostly about the probability of price events in the future. If the likeliness of an event to occur is very high, then the option that would be profiting from that event will be more expensive. Options contracts also come with expiration dates. The lesser the time until the date of expiration, the value of the option will be less too. This is because as we come closer to the date of expiration, any chances of the significant price movement of the underlying security start to reduce. Thus, with time, the option ultimately becomes a wasting asset. The risk associated with trading options is always limited to the price of the option, and hence there is no margin requirement here.

I will explain options trading in detail with examples in the next chapter. Until then, there are some key terminologies that you should know about. Without these, you should never step into the world of options trading.

Some Key Terms That You Should Know About

- **Strike Price** – You will see the term strike price being used very often. But what does it mean? The price at which the options contract can be sold or purchased is known as the strike price. The determination of the value of an option is done with the help of its strike price, along with several other factors.

- **Expiration Date** – Yes, options come with expiration dates! The owner of the option will have to decide what they want to do with the contract before the expiration date, after which it will become worthless. They can either choose to realize the profits or the loss by closing the position, or they can exercise the option, or they can choose to let it expire worthless.

- **Option Premium** – The option contract's current market price is its option premium.

Why is Options Trading Worth the Risk?

Trading options can help you earn some good profits, but there are also significant risk factors involved, so is it worth the risk? Well, we are going to discuss that in this section. Firstly, I'd like you to get one thing straight – options trading are of different types, and each type has a different set of risk factors associated with it. So, not every type of option trading is as risky as you think it is. Secondly, you also need to keep in mind that no matter what strategy you are using to trade options, if it is a good strategy, it will also consist of ways to reduce your risks to a minimum. But what makes options trading worth it after everything is the profit potential. So, let us have a look at some of the advantages and disadvantages of options trading, and then you can decide for yourself whether you are in for it or not.

Advantages

There are plenty of advantages that I can think of, but some of the major ones are listed below –

- The financial commitment in the case of buying shares directly is way more than options trading. You have to invest a lot of money in shares, but when you buy an option, the overall money required is, most of the time, much less than that of stocks.

- You are able to employ quite a huge amount of leverage in the case of options trading as compared to stocks. But this advantage applies only to the disciplined who know how to use leverage in a proper manner.

- You can take advantage of different market characteristics with the varied strategies of options trading. These strategies are quite unique and specially designed for you to profit out of time decay, volatility, and so on.

- The flexibility in the case of options trading is also much more.

Disadvantages

Now, let us have a look at some of the disadvantages of options that you need to be careful about –

- Time decay is one of the major disadvantages of options trading. As the options approach the date of expiration, their value keeps decreasing considerably.

- The commissions in options trading are usually more.

- For beginners, options trading might seem more complicated than stocks.

- A good number of stocks are available in the form of options, but you will not get options for every stock in the market.

Styles of Options

There are two major styles of options that you should know about, and most of the options that you possess will fall under either of these two –

- **American Options** – These are a specific type of options contract where you can choose to exercise the rights either on the date of expiration or before that. Thus, as soon as you see that your prediction is true and the underlying stock's movement is favorable to you, you can capture your profits.

European Options – Then, we have another type of options contract known as the European options. Here, the right to exercise the option belongs to the holder of the contract has the right to exercise their rights only on the date of expiration and not on any other date. Contrary to popular misconception, these two options have nothing to do with where these two places are located on earth.

Chapter 2

Getting Started With Options Trading

Before you jump right into the depths of options trading and learn the various strategies, you first have to have a clear concept of the basics. To be honest, only the sky is the limit when it comes to learning new things. Options are just one of the many ways through which you can earn some handsome profits in the stock market. Options might seem a bit complicated at first, but with the right guidance, it will start becoming easier. So, without any further ado, let's dive right in.

Types of Options

The two types of options contracts that you should know about have been described below –

Call Option

This is a specific type of options contract where the owner of the contract has the right to purchase a security but is not obligated to do so, and this purchase will be made at a specific price. This price that we are talking about is also popularly known as the strike price of the option. Moreover, the transaction has to be done within particular expiration date. The option premium is what you pay in order to purchase a call option. Whether the holder of the options contract wants to exercise the option or not is entirely in their hands, and they are under no obligation to exercise if they don't want to. If the person thinks that exercising the option would only be unprofitable, then they can choose to let it expire worthless. On the contrary, the seller will be under the obligation to sell the underlying securities that the buyer wants. The losses in a call option are capped to the total option premium you paid at the time of purchase, and at the same time, the profit potential here has no limits.

The call options can be further divided into three different types –

- **In-the-money** – In these options, the strike price of the option is always more than the underlying security's price.

- **At-the-money** – This is when the strike is equal to the underlying security's price.

- **Out-of-the-money** – Here, the underlying security's price is always lower than the option's strike price.

The call options should become even clearer to you once you go through this example mentioned below –

Let us assume that an investor selects the stock of a particular company ABC and purchases a call option at $10, which is its strike price. If the person speculates that there is going to be an increase in the underlying stock's price, then the investor stands to make a profit because they purchased the options contract at a lower price slab and will be selling at a price slab higher than that provided the rise in price happens before the expiration date. But exercising the option would be fruitful for the buyer only if the strike price is at a slab lower than that of the present price in the market. For example, if the underlying security is now trading at $8, then it would be a loss to exercise the option.

Put Option

Now, we are going to discuss the second type of options – the put options. They are the complete opposite of call options. The person who holds the contract of the put options has the right to sell the underlying security before the date of expiration at a specific price. Investors get the chance to lock a certain minimum price when it comes to selling the underlying security. Just like the call options, there is no obligation on the holder of the option to exercise it. In case the price in the market is more than the option's strike price, the investor can simply opt for keeping the option as it is and not exercise it.

Here too, there are three different in which put options can be categorized, and you should definitely have a basic knowledge about these –

- **In-the-money** – In this case, the options contract's strike price is more than that of the underlying security's price.

- **At-the-money** – In these options contracts, the underlying security's price is the same as the strike price.

- **Out-of-the-money** – Here, the options contract's strike price is lesser than that of the underlying security's price.

An example would help you understand put options better. Let us assume that the investor has selected the stocks of an ABC company and purchases the put option at $10, which is the strike price. If the underlying stock's present price in the market is lesser than that of the options contract's strike price, only then would it be fruitful for the investor to go along and make the decision of exercising the option. On the other hand, in case the stock's price increases to $11, then it is not advisable or profitable for the investor to sell the options contract at $10.

Now, we are going to discuss some other types of options as well.

Exchange-Traded Option

These options are also known by the term listed options, and these are considered to be very popular. These are options contracts that are traded at exchanges, and they are guaranteed. These trades are settled through a clearinghouse. One of the common names that you might know where trading of these options is done is the CBOE or the Chicago Board Options Exchange. There are specific regulators that oversee the functioning of these exchanges. These include the CFTC or the Commodity Futures Trading Commission and SEC or the Securities and Exchange Commission. A very popular clearinghouse that oversees the operations is OCC or Options Clearing Corporation.

Over the Counter Options or OTC

The options falling under this category are the ones that are traded in specifically OTC markets. They are not traded in any formal exchanges. In simpler terms, these are exotic options, and they are also private transactions between the seller and the buyer. There is no standardization of expiration dates or strike prices here, so the terms are decided by the participants themselves. Many investors find these options attractive because of the endless flexibility involved. Since there are no disclosure requirements, there is always a risk that the contractual obligations will not be fulfilled by the counterparties. An offsetting transaction is created to close these options position since there is no secondary market here.

Options Based on Underlying Securities

We can also divide the options depending on the underlying security involved, and we are going to discuss them in brief here –

- **Stock options** – These are probably the most common types of options. As you can understand from the term, the underlying security here are stocks, that is, shares of a company that are publicly traded.

- **Index options** – They have a similarity with that of stock options, but here, it is indexes that form the underlying asset. Thus, the stocks of companies that are included here belong to a certain index, for example, the S&P 500.

- **Commodity options** – Then, there are commodity options where the underlying security can be either a physical commodity or a futures contract.

- **Forex/Currency options** – After the stock options, a popular category of options are the currency options, with the help of which the investor acquires the right to sell or purchase any specific currency at a set exchange rate as mentioned in the contract.

- **Basket options** – Here, the underlying securities are a group of things and, thus, the name basket options. Any combination of financial instruments can form this basket, for example, commodities, stocks, currencies, and so on.

Options Based on Their Expiration Cycle

Another method of categorizing options is through their expiration cycle.

- **Regular options** – This is your standard type of options contract where there is one expiration cycle. When you purchase these options contracts, you can select your expiration from four different months. The choice will depend entirely on your preference.

- **Weekly options** – These are very similar to regular options, but the only difference is that the period of expiration is way shorter.

- **LEAPS** – This is the acronym for Long-Term Expiration Anticipation Securities, and their system is that their expiration date is always fixed in the month of January. Thus the period of expiration can be anywhere between one to three years and is thus, meant for long-term options trading.

Now, let us discuss some other options in the miscellaneous category.

Employee Stock Options

These are a special category of options where the employees of a company obtain the right to buy the shares of a company in a specific number and within a certain period of time and at a specific price. Both private and public sector companies are using these options nowadays, mainly because they want to attract more employees. This strategy is also used to compensate the employees and increase the employee retention rate. You have to keep in mind that these types of options are not the same as options that are sold or purchased by traders at the exchange. These are mostly in the form of call options because the employee acquires the right to purchase, and then, the person can choose to exercise the option before the expiration date at a certain strike price.

Cash-Settled Options

They are a separate category of options where the form of settlement is different than the other types. Usually, the underlying securities are transferred, and that is how the contract is settled. But here, that doesn't happen. These contracts can be settled only through cash. The holder of the security will be receiving the profit in cash from the writer of the contract. But when are these options mostly used? They are mainly used in situations where the underlying security is not so liquid and is thus, costly or difficult to transfer.

Exotic Options

Compared to the options that are usually traded, this one is quite complex. You will not find these options in the usual stock exchanges because they are most traded in OTC markets. They can be customized and are thus, non-standardized. But since these types of options are now rising in popularity, there are some types that are available on exchanges, too, for example, compound options, barrier options, binary options, and so on.

Intrinsic Value and Time Value of Options

If you want to enter the world of options trading, there's another concept that is very crucial for you to grasp, and that is the intrinsic and time value of options and why they matter.

You have already heard of the term option premium, but do you know what it comprises of? The value of an option consists of two different numbers. The first one is the intrinsic value which is the current value of an options contract and the second one is the time value which is the potential increase in value over time that could happen to an option. Now, we are going to study both these components in detail.

Intrinsic Value

With the intrinsic value of an option, you get to know how much in-the-money the option really is. In simpler words, the buyer will have a positive payoff when they have an in-the-money option. If a call option is $30 and the underlying security has a price of $40, then the option is said to be in-the-money by $10. If this particular option is then exercised by the buyer at this point, then the stock can be bought at $30, and then he can sell the stock in the market for $40 making a profit of $10. So, you see, the payoff that the buyer would receive in case he decides to exercise the option is what the intrinsic value represents.

On the contrary, the intrinsic value of an option is considered to be zero for options that are at-the-money or out-of-the-money. This is because in the event these options are exercised by the buyer, he would not make a profit and, in turn, incur a loss. So, the buyer should allow the option to expire worthless and thus receive no payoff.

Time Value

Any additional amount on top of the current intrinsic value that is paid by the investor is known as time value. When there is a chance that the option will witness an increase in value before it reaches expiration, then the investors are willing to pay this price. So, if an option still has months left to expire, then the time value has more chances to be high because there is still a lot of time left for the option to increase in value as compared to an option contract whose expiration is within a few weeks or days. Similarly, the time value of an option that is expiring today is extremely low or almost nil because there is a negligible chance for the option to witness an increase in its value before expiration.

Why Do These Values Matter?

Now, let us come to the most important question, why do you think these values matter? For starters, they help to make purchase decisions because, with the help of these values, any investor can analyze what they are paying. In simpler terms, the investor will have a better idea about the risk and reward associated with an option.

The chances of an option expiring worthless on the date of expiration are way more if the investor has bought an at-the-money or out-of-the-money option, and the time value and premium of the option are the same. Similarly, when a person is purchasing an option that is in-the-money, then the chances of that option expiring worthless are way less since the option already holds a lot of value. The premium of such options is also high because they have not only the intrinsic value but also the time value added to it.

Buying/Selling Call Options

Do you know what the main advantage of buying a call option is? The increase in the stock price is magnified! At the same time, the upfront cost that you have to bear is very low, and until the option reaches the expiration date, you keep enjoying the profits above the strike price. So, any person who is purchasing a call option must have speculated a rise in the price of the underlying security before the option reaches the expiration date.

But first, you need to find the right call options to buy. There are few things to keep in mind for doing that –

- The amount of money you want to spend in purchasing the call option

- The time span for which you want to stay in the trade

- Your expectation for the length of the market's move

If your speculation for the underlying security is that it will complete its movement towards the higher side in two weeks, then you should purchase an option that will have at least two weeks' time in its expiration. Similarly, if you plan to be in the trade for only two to three weeks, then you should not buy options whose expiration is in six or nine months or more. In that case, you will lose leverage, and you will have to shell out a huge chunk of money because these options will be expensive.

Another thing to keep in mind is that in the last thirty days of expiration, the time value of an option decays way faster. So, even if your assumptions are correct and you don't factor in time decay, in the end, you might still end up with a loss. So, my suggestion would be to always go for options where you expect that you will be in the trade for more than thirty days.

Your tolerance towards risk and your account size will determine how much amount you can set aside for purchasing a call option. Taking these factors into account, sometimes, you might find that certain options are being too costly for you. In fact, at times, you might find that the options you are looking at are not at all the right choice for you. In the case of options, the premium has to be entirely paid upfront, so you might end up paying thousands of dollars in certain volatile markets. A very common example is that of crude oil. Such markets are not meant for every type of trader, and don't give in to your temptation because if you end up buying deep out-of-the-money options just because you can afford them, the chances of those options expiring worthlessly are way higher.

Here are some key points that you need to keep in mind with respect to the payoff received by the call options buyer –

- The total premium paid by the buyer to purchase the call option is the maximum loss that he can incur from the transaction. As long as the strike price is above the spot price, the buyer will face a loss.

- The profit potential for the buyer of the call options is unlimited because you don't know how much higher the spot price can move above the strike price.

- It is true that when the spot price starts moving above the strike price, the buyer of the call option stands to make a profit. But you also have to keep in mind that the buyer will first have to cover the premium he already paid.

- The breakeven point is reached in the trade when the buyer has completely recovered the total premium he paid in purchasing the call option.

- It is beyond this breakeven point that the true profit starts accumulating for the call option buyer.

Now, let us talk about selling a call option. Options buyer and sellers are like two sides of the same coin. But what happens to the options buyer does not happen to the seller. Instead, the exact opposite happens in the case of the seller. For example, if the buyer stands to make $10 in profits from a trade, then the seller is losing $10 in that same trade.

First, you need to be clear about a very basic concept. When someone is selling a call option, that person is giving the right to purchase the underlying security to the buyer, and this has to be done within a set date of expiration and at a specific price. This also means that no matter which direction the market goes, if the buyer decides to act now, the seller will be under the obligation to sell the underlying security at the strike price that was decided.

There are two ways in which a call option can be sold, and we are going to discuss them briefly here –

- **Covered call option –** You already know that the call option is based on the underlying security and when the seller owns that security, in that case, it is called a covered call. These are considered to be of the low-risk type because the underlying security has already been purchased by the seller at a price that is lower than the strike price. This means that the seller is covered or protected by the premium in case there is a loss (when the buyer chooses to purchase the call option). The seller will have a chance of losing out on a huge profit even if they do not lose any actual money.

- **Short or naked call option –** This is exactly the opposite of a covered call where the seller does not own the underlying security. The risk involved in this type of call option is considerably higher because there is no limit to the price of the underlying security, and since the seller does not have any ownership here, he is not protected.

But why will you sell a call option? Two of the most popular reasons why people prefer selling call options are –

- There is a much-controlled risk.
- Futures and shares don't usually crash up.

There is risk associated with all forms of trading, and there is no two way about it. But in case there is a loss by selling a call option, there is no big stress factor here for the seller because he is not going to lose any significant assets. Moreover, in case the market is crashing up, selling the call options would also ensure that you are not forcefully made to exit the market position. But there is always the fear of a downward crash, so you might still incur an unlimited loss. The catch is that such an event rarely happens, and on the plus side, there is no downside tail-risk, so selling call options is a much safer bet.

Buying/Selling Put Options

The difference between call and put options is the way in which a person views the markets. For the buyer of a put option, he is anticipating that the price of the underlying security is going to go down. So, as the price falls, the buyer will make money. The best thing about puts is the fact that with only a small move in the price of the stock, they can appreciate very fast. Thus, anyone who believes in making huge profits in a small span of the time prefers the put options.

The trader is paying a very small amount in the beginning, and he is profiting from the decline in the price of the underlying security below the strike price until the option reaches its expiration date.

Here are some key things to know about the payoff of a put option buyer –

- When the strike price is below the spot price, that is when the buyer of the put option experiences a loss.

- The loss is, however, limited, and it is capped at the total premium paid by the trader.

- When the strike price is above the spot price, the buyer of the put option experiences an exponential gain.

- The profit potential of the buyer is unlimited here.

- The put option buyer will not lose money or make any profit at the breakeven point.

Investors can secure a profit from the selling of put options as well. The idea is to profit from the premium received for the option once the options lose value. The seller is always under the obligation to sell the underlying security once the puts have been sold to a buyer and the buyer chooses to exercise the option. In order to incur a profit, the price of the underlying security must go above the strike price or remain equal to it.

Call Spreads

As you might know, the spreads are essentially a multi-leg approach to profit from a trade-in multiple ways. In this section, we are going to discuss both the bull call spread and the bear call spread.

Bull Call Spread

The main aim of the bull call spread is to make a profit from a gradual increase in the price of the underlying security. This strategy is meant for traders who expect a rise in the price of the underlying security and are moderately bullish on it.

Here's what you have to do in order to implement this strategy –

- Buy one at-the-money call option

- Sell one out-of-the-money call option

But there are also some things to keep in mind –

- When you are selling or purchasing the call options, they should belong to the same underlying security.

- They should have the same expiration date.

- Each leg of this strategy should comprise the same number of options.

- There is no profit or loss at the breakeven point. In this case, the breakeven point is calculated by adding the net debit and lower strike.

- There is a limited loss.

- The profit is also limited.

So, what is the maximum profit? You have to subtract the commissions from the difference between the strike prices, and you will get your maximum profit. But the scenario of maximum profit can be reached only if the strike price is at the same level or less than the price of the underlying security at the time of expiration.

And the maximum risk in the bull call spread is the total commissions paid along with the cost of the spread. You will face this situation if both the call options you purchased expire worthlessly on the date of expiration. This happens when the strike price of the long call option is above the price of the underlying security or asset.

Bear Call Spread

This is also a two-leg strategy, just like what you saw in the bull call spread, but the only difference is that this strategy is followed when you speculate the market to be moderately bearish. In terms of the payoff, both the strategies are very similar to each other, but the difference lies mostly in the strike selection and execution of the strategy.

In order to build this strategy, you will have to –

- Buy a short call option

- Sell a long call option

Things to keep in mind in this strategy are as follows –

- Both the call options involved in this strategy should have the same underlying asset.

- Their expiration dates should also be the same.

- The profit in a bear call spread is achieved by time erosion or a declining stock, or both.

- The potential for loss is limited.

- The profit potential is also limited.

The maximum profit that can be made from this strategy is found out by subtracting the commissions you paid from the net premium you received. The situation of profit will arrive when at the time of expiration, the short call's strike price is above the price of the underlying security. If this happens, then both the call options will expire worthlessly, and you will profit from it.

Similarly, the maximum risk involved can be calculated by subtracting the net credit you received from the difference between the strike prices. This risk will be realized by the trader in situations where the strike price of the long call is lower than the price of the underlying asset at the time of expiration.

The Long Straddle

There are times in every trader's life when after extensive planning, the market goes in a completely different direction due to some unforeseen circumstance, and all your capital and effort go to waste. But there are strategies that can give you insulation for such conditions. When the profitability of a strategy is not dependent on which direction the market moves, such strategies are termed as delta neutral or market strategies, and the long straddle is one of them.

Among the different neutral strategies, this is the easiest one. A positive P&L will be produced as long as the market keeps moving no matter what the direction is.

In order to implement this strategy, this is what you need to do –

- Purchase a call option
- Purchase a put option

Things that you need to ensure are –

- The options that you are purchasing should have the same underlying security.

- They should have the same date of expiration.

- The strike price should be the same.

On the upside, the potential for profit is unlimited because there is no end to how much the price of the underlying asset can rise. And, on the downside, there is substantial profit potential since the price of the underlying asset can reduce to zero.

The maximum risk that you can incur with this strategy is capped to the total cost of building this strategy, along with the commissions that you have to pay. The loss will happen in a situation where both options expire worthlessly. This happens when the strike price and the price of the underlying asset are the same on the date of expiration.

Since the cost of your position is considerably increased in this strategy, in order to break even, the price swing needs to be quite significant. If traders speculate an increase in implied volatility, that is when they run this strategy. So, the idea time for this strategy is when you think there will be a big price change in an asset irrespective of the direction.

The Long Strangle

This is also a neutral strategy, and here too, your goal is to make a profit from a market move irrespective of the direction of the move. The difference between a long straddle and long strangles is that in the former, the strike prices were the same, and in the latter, the strike prices are different.

Here too, if you want to build this strategy, you will have to –

- Purchase a slightly out-of-the-money call with a higher strike price

- Purchase a slightly out-of-the-money put with a lower strike price

Things to keep in mind to fulfill this strategy are –

- The underlying asset for both options is the same.

- The expiration date is also the same.

- The strike price for both options will be different.

On the upside, the potential for profit is unlimited because there can be an indefinite increase in the price of the underlying asset. On the downside, there is substantial potential for profit as well because the price of the underlying asset can reduce to zero.

The potential loss in this strategy is limited too and is equal to the commissions you paid along with the cost of the strangle. You will realize this loss if both your options expire worthlessly.

At expiration, there are two possible breakeven points –

- The first is the total premium plus higher strike price
- The second one is the lower strike price minus the total premium you paid

Since both the put and the call option you purchased are slightly out-of-the-money, in order to make a profit, the market move has to be quite substantial. So, conditions of high volatility are perfect for playing this strategy.

Technical Analysis

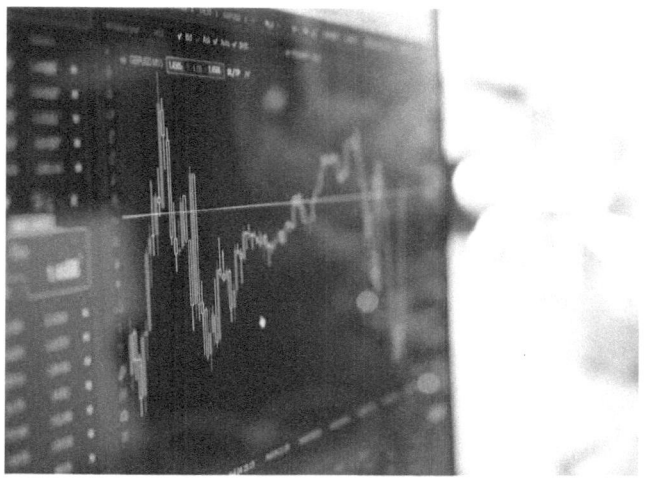

Both technical and fundamental analysis is important when it comes to the stock market, but since options trading is done mostly in the short-term, technical analysis plays a big role here. Any standard options will not depend on fundamental analysis because they are not going to last that long. So, if you want to figure out your entry and exit points in a trade or what the market sentiment is going to be, technical analysis will be your best friend. In this section, we are going to learn about some of the major technical indicators that you need to know about if you want to excel at options trading.

Support and Resistance Levels

These levels are usually used by analysts to find out where would be the point of reversal for a prevailing trend or whether the prevailing trend would make a pause at a certain point. Support occurs when the demand becomes too concentrated, and there is a pause in the downtrend. Similarly, resistance occurs when the supply is concentrated, and there is a temporary pause in the uptrend. Since everyone in the market is trying to speculate the future movements, their decisions are influenced by what happened in the past, and thus, market psychology is of huge importance here.

Once you have found out the resistance or support zones on the chart, you can consider those points as your entry or exit from a trade. This is important because when the price reaches these levels, either of these two things is going to happen –

- Not maintain the price level and keep going in the same direction

- Bounce away from these levels

This will continue until the price finds the next resistance or support levels on the chart. Sometimes traders have faith that these levels will not be broken, and that is how they decide the timing of their trades.

RSI or Relative Strength Index

Next, we come to another very important technical indicator used in options trading. You can predict the price of the underlying security before there is any movement with the help of this indicator. The oversold and overbought conditions are identified with the help of the RSI. When the value of RSI is above 70, it is considered to be overbought, and on the other hand, when the value is below 30, it is considered to be oversold. The value can range only between 0 and 100. But these levels are not stringent. Depending on the security and the situation, the levels are adjusted. For example, if the overbought level is being tapped by the security multiple times, then the level of RSI might be adjusted to 80. If the trend is strong, then the oversold or overbought state might continue for a long duration of time.

But the usage of RSI is more accurate and suitable when you are dealing with options on individual stocks as compared to other securities like indexes because the oversold and overbought conditions are more commonly seen in stocks than indexes. If you are going to use RSI for short-term trading, then your best bet is to use them on high-beta stocks that are highly liquid.

Bollinger Bands

This technical indicator is not exactly used to pinpoint a particular zone to sell or buy your stock, but it is more about finding out the volatility. The importance of volatility in trading cannot be explained in words. When the volatility increases, these bands increase, and when the volatility decreases, the bands contract. The underlying asset is considered to be overbought if the price of the asset moves closer to the upper band. Similarly, the condition is said to be oversold if the price of the underlying asset starts to move closer to the lower band.

You can speculate a reversal if there is any price movement outside of these bands. And then, you can decide your positions based on your speculation.

In general, an important tip to keep in mind is that when there is high volatility in the market, it is advisable to sell your options because the price of these options is elevated. Similarly, when the volatility is low, it is best to buy options because of the decrease in price.

IMI or Intraday Momentum Index

If you are someone who is looking for intraday moves to make money, then this technical indicator is going to be your best friend. When the market is up-trending, the IMI will help you initiate a bullish trade by finding suitable opportunities for the same. Similarly, it will help you spot an intraday price bump in a bearish market so that you can engage in a bearish trade.

Apart from the technical indicators that I have mentioned above, there are several others, for example, MFI or money flow index, average true range, stochastic oscillators, and so on. The technical indicator that you should use depends on various factors like your risk appetite, your strategy, and your trading style.

Chapter 3

The Greeks

There are many factors that can influence the price of an option, and all of these factors will help you to decide your positions during a trade. The Greeks are a set of risk measures that are included in these factors that affect the option pricing. Each of these risk measures is denoted by a Greek letter and hence the name. In this chapter, we are going to study each of the Greeks in detail.

Delta

Delta is also popularly known as the hedge ratio. In simpler terms, it will help you measure the expected change in the price of an option with respect to per $1 change in the price of the underlying index or security. Firstly, I'd like to remind you that when you trade options, it is very important for you to set realistic expectations on the price behavior.

For call options:

Delta has a positive value for call options, and its value can be anything between 0.0 to 1.00. The value of Delta is usually near 0.50 for options that are at-the-money. The more the option gets deeper-in-the-money, the more will be the increase in the value of the Delta.

For put options:

Delta has a negative value for put options with a range of 0.0 to -1.00. The Delta value of options that are at-the-money is usually near -0.50. The more the option gets deeper-in-the-money, the more will be the decrease in the value of the option.

In fact, you can also see Delta as a probability. It signified how much chance does any given option has that it will expire in-the-money. So, if the Delta value of any option is 0.50, then it means that at the time of expiration, there is a 50% chance for that option to be in-the-money. But remember that this is not an indicator of whether your trade will be profitable or not. The potential for profit will obviously depend on how much did you sold or bought the option for.

Another way in which Delta is used is to figure out directional risk. When the value of the Delta is positive, those are long market assumptions. Similarly, it denotes short market assumptions when the value of the Delta is negative. And neutral market assumptions are made by neutral delta values.

Gamma

For ease of understanding, keep in mind that Gamma denotes the rate at which the value of Delta changes. So, the rate of change of the value of Delta of an option for every $1 change in the price of the underlying asset is what Gamma stands for. So, if you correlate this with high-school physics, then Delta is 'speed,' and Gamma is 'acceleration.'

The price of the underlying asset is what determines the change in the value of Delta; Gamma is used for measuring how stable Delta is by representing its rate of change.

An example should make this clearer to you. Let us assume that there are two options – both of these options have the same Delta value. But the Gamma value of one of these options is higher than the other. Then, there will be a higher risk associated with the option having a high Gamma value. This is because if there is any movement in the price of the underlying security that is unfavorable to you, then the impact of that move will also be huge. In simpler words, there is a lot of volatility in options that have a higher Gamma value. So, if you are looking for a trade where you have predictable opportunities, then such options are not ideal for you.

Also, the value of the Gamma is at its highest when the option gets near the money. For options that are deep-in-the-money and deep out-of-the-money, the value of Gamma is the lowest. For short options, the Gamma value is negative, and for long options, the Gamma value is positive.

Theta

Next, we come to Theta, which is also known as time decay. For an option buyer, Theta is the number one enemy. On the contrary, for an option seller, Theta is their best friend. For a single-day change in time until the date of expiration, the decrease in the price of puts and calls is measured by Theta. We all know that the value of options starts decreasing as the date of expiration comes near. And Theta quantifies that loss in value and tells you how much decrease in value will happen in one day, considering all other factors remain the same.

As the option keeps approaching its date of expiration, its chances of fetching you some good returns in-the-money become even far less probable. Since the time to earn profit reduces, the time decay starts accelerating with an approaching date of expiration. If you consider a single option, then the value of Theta is always found to be negative since the direction of movement of time is the same. The clock will start ticking the moment an option is purchased by the trader until the date of expiration.

Vega

This Greek factor measures the sensitivity to volatility. It helps to measure the change in the prices of calls and puts for a subsequent one-point change in the implied volatility. Remember that the intrinsic value of an option has nothing to do with Vega and is thus, not affected by it as well. The option price's time value is what is affected here. In a general situation, there will be an increase in the value of an option if there is an increase in implied volatility. This is because when implied volatility increases, there are high chances that the stock would undergo an increased range of movement.

When you are trying to determine the value of any option, one of the major factors to consider is volatility, and this makes Vega a very important factor to consider. Both the puts and calls will undergo a loss in value if the Vega decreases. Similarly, both puts and calls will increase in value if there is an increase in Vega.

If you do not take Vega seriously as most beginners do, you might end up paying an unnecessarily huge amount of money for buying options. If we are considering a general situation where other factors are constant, then it is safe to say when the value of Vega is below the normal standard, then you should purchase options. And, when the value of Vega is above the normal standard, then you should sell options. If the option is getting closer to its date of expiration, then there will be a decrease in the value of Vega.

Rho

Another major Greek is Rho, with the help of which you can measure the change in the price of the option for every one percent change in the rate of interest. When it comes to analyzing the price of an option, Rho is usually a very crucial factor, but you should be considering it only if you speculate that the interest rates that are prevailing might undergo a change. Short-term options are not usually sensitive to interest rates, but on the other hand, LEAPS are highly sensitive to them.

Minor Greeks

You might sometimes come across a term known as minor Greeks. They are not so frequently discussed. Some minor Greeks include ultima, color, zomma, speed, vomma, and lambda. If you see the pricing model, these Greeks usually comprise the third or second derivatives, so they mostly affect volatility or the change in Delta. These Greeks are not being used more and more in trading because the software on computers can perform complex calculations within a few seconds and produce accurate results.

Let me give you a brief idea of what some of these Greeks represent –

- **Lambda** – With the help of this Greek factor, you will be able to assess that with an increase in the price of the option, how much leverage is it providing you. Thus, you might even find this factor is referred to as the leverage factor.

- **Vomma** – The reaction showed by Vega to the change in volatility is measured by vomma. So, if you can use Vega and Vomma together in a proper manner, you can easily find out the profitability of your trades.

- **Zomma** – This is a third-order derivative that will help you figure out how sensitive the Gamma value of an options contract is when the implied volatility of the contract undergoes a change.

So, as you can see in this chapter, all the Greek variables that are present will show you how the price of the option is affected when some underlying variable changes.

Chapter 4

Swing Trading with Options

In this chapter, we are going to learn every detail about the swing trading strategy in options trading. It is quite uncomplicated, and it will help you bring home profits quickly and in a smart way. Before we move on to the details, I will like to share with you three major benefits that you are going to enjoy by indulging in the swing trading technique –

- With an initial investment, earn significant profits.

- Your risk exposure becomes limited.

- Even if you have a small account, you can trade in high-price stocks.

For leveraging your initial investment, options are a very good choice when it comes to swing trading. Even if you want to trade with the best options in swing trading, for example, the so-called expensive stocks like that of Amazon, you will not have to put in much capital.

Moreover, this strategy is mainly about puts and calls options. Irrespective of the range or depth, with swing trading, you can make the best out of short-term stock shocks. Let us say that a certain stock is facing sudden volatility, then the options' value will hit the ceiling.

In fact, when the trading sessions are explosive, there have been past instances where options that were out-of-the-money quadrupled overnight. Now, let us move into some of the details of swing trading.

What is Swing Trading?

In this section, we are going to give you a better picture of what swing trading is. It is a special strategy where you make the best of short-term trends and make smaller gains by cutting your losses in a quicker fashion. Even though the gains are smaller, if you keep making these gains consistently over a period of time, your annual returns will be very good.

Support and Resistance Secrets

One of the main aspects of technical analysis is support and resistance levels. If you have a better grasp of these two concepts then, you can easily build a full-proof swing trading strategy with ease.

A support level can be identified on the graph by finding that area or zone where the current market price is above the price of the underlying asset, and thus, the selling pressure can be overcome by the buying pressure. Because of such an occurrence, you will see a reversal in the decrease of the price, and the price will start moving back up. Your aim is to enter a buy trade when you notice that there is a bounce from the support line. The idea position to place your stop loss, in this case, would be just below the line of support.

As far as resistance is concerned, the concept is exactly the opposite of that of support. In order to identify the resistance level on the graph, find a region on top of the current market price where the buying pressure has been overcome by the selling pressure. As a result of this, the price has reversed and started going back down. When such a situation occurs, the trader should enter a sell position. This has to be done at the point the price bounces back from the resistance level. You also need a stop loss, and it has to be placed just on top of the resistance line.

But there is a very important thing that traders often forget – if the price breaks through either of these levels, then the support and resistance levels switch roles. Thus, what was support initially, now becomes the resistance, and what was resistance becomes support.

Difference Between Trend Trader and Swing Trader

All the strategies that we see in the world of trading are either in the category of swing trading or trend trading. So, what are you? A trend trader or a swing trader? To understand that, let us evaluate both in some detail.

Both the types of strategies have their own requirements to be met and their own disadvantages and advantages as well. But some investors think that they can just go and apply any one of these, and they will still make a profit. That's not how things happen and if you are doing this, remember that you are only undermining your potential to make more profit. If you want to hone your skills and your strategy the right way, then you have to figure out whether you are a swing trader or a trend trader.

Theoretically speaking, you will often find trend traders taking risks in times of a downtrend or an uptrend, and until and unless that trend changes, they stay positioned in the same place. Alternatively, a swing trader has range-bound markets, and they perform their operation within those boundaries, selling at resistance and buying at support.

If you want to trade for a short duration of time, then swing trading will work better for you, but on the other hand, when you want to trade for months, then the trend-following strategies are your best friend. But ever since the advent of real-time charting, the lines have really become blurred.

If you are new to the market, then it's better if you choose one of these styles, master it, and then move on to the other one. If you have been in the market for quite some time and gained sufficient experience, then you can mix and match these approaches all you want. In such cases, the result is usually great, but in order to carry out such hybrids, you also need a lot of discipline that comes with experience.

Going Long on a Stock

You will often hear the phrase 'going long on a stock' when you come into the world of trading, but what do long positions really mean? In this section, we are going to elaborate on it. A long position is when a trader speculates that there will be a rise in the price of an underlying asset, and so they buy it. In options, it means that the holder actually owns the underlying security.

In very simple terms, when you are holding a long position, your view of the market is bullish. A short position and a long position are complete opposites of each other. When someone is buying an options contract, the term long position is used quite frequently. Depending on the outlook the trader has, he can hold on to the long put or long call option.

Here's an example to make this even clearer – let us assume that an investor speculates an upward movement in the price of the underlying security and hopes to profit from it; in that case, he will go long on a call option. When he does that, he acquires the right to purchase the underlying security at a certain specified price. On the other hand, if the investor speculates that there will be a fall in the price of the underlying asset, then he will go long on a put option. In that case, he will acquire the right to sell the underlying asset at a certain specified price. So, as you see, in the case of options trading, going long on a stock does not always signify a bullish sentiment. In the case of put options, it signifies a bearish sentiment.

How to Spot a Reversal Trend?

It is a lucrative opportunity for any trader to spot market reversal points. But for trend traders, one of the biggest fear is that they don't want to get caught in this market reversal. But what is a reversal? As you can guess from the term, a reversal is when the current trend of the underlying asset changes. When someone is able to spot these reversal points successfully, they can get out of the trades before it becomes completely unfavorable for them, and they suffer huge losses. You can even get into new trades when reversal signs come up because, at the time of the reversal, a new trend starts.

There are technical indicators that will help you identify a reversal trend, for example, moving averages, volume oscillator, and so on. But without these, too, there are some observations that you can make to spot a reversal in trend.

When there is a healthy uptrend, you will mostly find that it constitutes bullish candles rather than bearish candles. The bearish candles are relatively shorter in size compared to the bullish ones. Moreover, you will find that the bullish candles are closing towards the highs. But you can conclude that weakness in buying pressure is arising when you find that the bullish candles are gradually becoming shorter. It can also mean that an equal amount of selling pressure is coming into the market. However, you have to keep in mind that this, in no way, says that the market is going to collapse lower. You should only treat it as a sign that there is a weakness taking root in buyers, and before they go up any higher, they might need to take a break.

Now, you need to understand another very important term that is related to the concept of market reversal – and that is – retracement. Simply put, there is always a weaker leg of any trend that is acting opposite to it, and it is known as a retracement. This move is mostly comprised of bearish candles than bullish ones. You will see that the bearish candles are closing towards either the lows or middle of the range. You can conclude that there is an increase in the selling pressure when you notice that the bearish candles are increasing in size. This means that the buyers are not interested in paying a higher price for underlying assets. Just like the previous example, this one, too, does not guarantee that there will be a reversal, but it definitely suggests that weakness is rising in the buyers.

As the trend keeps progressing and maturing, there will come the point of equilibrium which is also known as the distribution stage, and the buyers and sellers are at the same level. Here, the support level plays a crucial part because, for the buyers, it acts as their last hope and line of defense. Everyone who has a bullish trade will fall out if the support level breaks at this point. From my experience, I can give you a small tip – if, within a very short span of time, the support is tested multiple times, then its chances of breaking are much more.

How to Short a Stock With Options?

If you read newspapers or watch news about options trading, you will often find that short selling is being painted in a bad light. In fact, you might even find people blaming short-selling for someone's bankruptcy. But are all of these accusations true? Well, if you ask me, such unfortunate situations happen because the trader was not careful with his risk exposure and has implemented either zero or very poor risk management techniques.

So, coming to the topic, what does it actually mean to short a stock?

We all know the concept where you make money from an asset when its price rises but shorting a stock is all about making money when the price of the stock falls. So, here, you have to first sell the stock, and then, when the price declines, you buy it back at a much lower price than you had initially bough it. This will fetch you a profit if everything else goes according to plan. But did you know that you can short a stock with options as well? Yes, it can be done, but there are certain things that will be different here.

For starters, you know that options contracts come with an expiration date. So, the short position has to arrive before the option expires; otherwise, you won't be making any profit. When the date of expiration comes, you either have to follow through with all the obligations that the contract requires you to, or you can simply close the position too. So, if you have short-term bearish speculation, then it is profitable for you to short sell a stock with options.

Understanding a Candlestick Chart

The origin of candlestick charts goes way back a century in Japan. You can predict a short-term direction of price by studying and identifying different patterns that form on the candlestick chart. They offer a lot of information about the trade and hence, they are also quite popular among every type of trader.

Every candlestick that you see on the chart has four things that it denotes. It shows the open, low, high, and closing prices for the time span that has been chosen by the trader. The time span can be anything. You can select it as low as five minutes, or you can even set it to a day. The wide part of the candlesticks is referred to by a special term – 'real body.' The body represents the price range in that time period. When the open is higher than the close, then the body of the candlestick is shown all black. On the contrary, if the open was lower than the close, then the body of the candlestick is shown as empty.

However, these colors can all be altered and changed according to your preference on the trading platform.

Now, every candlestick pattern signified something different, and we are going to study the meaning of these patterns in this section. You can even identify the major resistance and support levels with the help of these candlestick patterns. You can even find new opportunities within the market and know when to exit a position. You will also get a greater insight into the pressures of buying and selling or identify conditions of market indecision.

Once a market downtrend is over, you will find bullish candlestick patterns emerging. This indicates that the price movement is going to reverse. They tell the traders that if you want to profit out of an upward trajectory, then you should think about going long. Now, we are going to discuss some of the very common bullish candlestick patterns.

Hammer

You can identify the hammer from its long wick on the lower side and a very small body. You will usually find the hammer at the lower portion of the downward trend.

When a hammer occurs, it means that a strong buying pressure came in and drove back the selling pressure. The colors, of course, can be different, but in general, compared to red hammers, green ones are indicators of a strong bullish market.

Inverse Hammer

This is another bullish pattern, and the difference between the inverse hammer and the hammer is that here, the lower wick is shorter in length while the upper wick is quite long.

When you find an inverse hammer, it denotes that there was a selling pressure right after the buying pressure, but the former was not strong enough to overcome the latter. The occurrence of this pattern also tells you or gives you the indication that the control of the market is soon going to be in the hands of the buyers.

Bullish Engulfing

This pattern involves not one but two candlesticks. There is a larger green candle that completely engulfs a shorter red candle. The red candle comes first. This pattern occurs when the sellers are outpaced by the buyers.

Morning Star

Just like its name, when the morning star candlestick pattern appears, it strikes the feeling of hope when the market is in a downtrend. There are a total of three sticks that form this pattern. There are one long green candle and one long red candle at the sides, and in the middle, there is a short candle. Generally, you will not find any overlap here. When you see this pattern, you can safely predict that the selling pressure has started reducing, and a bull market is coming soon.

Piercing Line

This is another two-stick candlestick pattern like you saw in bullish engulfing. Here, the first one is a long red candle, and after that, you will find a long green candle.

But if you notice the pattern closely, you will find that there is usually a gap between the closing price of the first candle and the opening price of the second candle, and the gap is quite significant. The occurrence of this pattern can be deciphered as an increase in buying pressure.

Three White Soldiers
This is a pattern that will take place over a span of three days. You can identify this pattern by consecutive long green candles or white candles, and all of them will have small wicks, and as you progress onto the next day, the wicks should open and close progressively.

This particular pattern is indicative of a strong bullish signal that denotes that the buying pressure is increasing steadily, and it is often spotted right after a downtrend.

Now that you have a basic idea of the bullish candlesticks, let us move on to the bearish ones, which are usually spotted when an uptrend ends. These are also indicative of resistance levels. Traders will start closing off their long positions if the market is filled with a pessimistic attitude towards the market price, and then, in order to make the best out of this falling price, traders open a short position.

Hanging Man
We discussed hammer in this chapter. It was a bullish pattern. The hanging man is often referred to as the equivalent of the hammer in the bearish market. The

shapes of both these patterns are the same, but the only difference is that you will find the hanging man forming at the bottom of an uptrend.

When you see the hanging man, it means that there was considerable selling pressure, but in the end, the buying pressure was so much that it pushed the price back up. This huge selling pressure is often concluded as the loss of control of the market for the bulls.

Shooting Star

Again, the inverted hammer and the shooting star have the same shape, but the formation of the shooting star is found in an uptrend. There will be a higher market gap at the time of opening, and before closing, it will reach an intra-day high, and then the closing price will be slightly on top of the open. All of this arrangement makes it appear like a star is falling to the ground, hence, the name shooting star.

Evening Star

This is another pattern that involves a total of three candlesticks. You read about the morning star pattern in the bullish section. Well, this is the equivalent of that, only it's in the bearish condition. There is a long green candle on one side, and on the other side, there is a long red candle and in between both of these is a short candle that appears to be sandwiched.

When this pattern appears, it means that the uptrend is going to reverse. Moreover, if you notice that the gains of the first candle have been erased by the third candle, then the reversal is quite strong.

Bearish Engulfing

At the bottom of the uptrend, you will find the bearish engulfing pattern. The small green candle appears first, and then comes the long red candle, which appears to be engulfing the smaller one.

It is predicted that the price movement will be slowed down or has reached a peak, and thus, there is a downturn coming. The trend will be stronger if the second candle goes even lower.

Three Black Crows

These consist of three candles side-by-side with very small or non-existent wicks. Every session opens, and then the selling pressure keeps increasing. So, even though they open at a somewhat similar price to the previous day, with each close, the price moves lower.

When you spot this pattern, you can safely assume that a downtrend is about to come.

CHAPTER 5

Iron Condor

The iron condor is a very special strategy in options trading where you use a four-legged approach. Here, you will be using both the put and call options. By now, you must have understood that there are plenty of options strategies that you can use in trading, and each of them has its own set of risks associated with them. Some are more risk-facing than others. At the same time, there are plenty of strategies that you can use to manage and reduce the risk exposure. The iron condor strategy is one such risk-management strategy. It is a special type of technique where you make the best use of the low volatility of the market. In this chapter, you will be learning more about the iron condor and in greater detail. So, without any further ado, let's dig in!

What is the Iron Condor?

The iron condor strategy is a special strategy that is used when the underlying asset is speculated to be in a condition of low volatility. It is a non-directional strategy with very limited risk. You can also see this strategy as an amalgamation of the bear call spread, and the bull put spread.

There are a total of four options involved in building this strategy, and something that all four of these have in common is that their expiration date is the same. So, if you want to proceed with this strategy, here's what you have to do –

- Sell an out-of-the-money call
- Sell an out-of-the-money put
- Purchase a further out-of-the-money call
- Purchase a further out-of-the-money put

Thus, these are the four legs that make up this strategy. In the end, you will have a net credit in your hands to put on the trade.

Understanding the Iron Condor

Now that you know how to build the iron condor and what it is, it's time you understand how it works in a bit more detail. An iron condor strategy is executed by traders who think that there won't be much price movement of the underlying asset. By executing this strategy, they get to collect a hefty premium. Moreover, the margin needed to create a vertical spread and the iron condor is the same, and thus, this strategy won't be much expensive to you even though you are creating two spreads here. But do you know why? Because no matter what happens, the trader will win at least one side in this trade.

Since the possibilities are great compared to the risk, the iron condor is a favorite among many traders, beginners, and experts alike. Anyone who executes this strategy has the hope that the trading range remains narrow so that the price of the option remains within the short strike prices on the day of expiration. Even if there are some bearish or bullish tendencies, this strategy can be executed, but that would depend on what the range is and what the relation to the price of the stock is.

In any case, if you decide to execute this strategy, my advice to you would be to close the position at least a couple of days before the date of expiration. This is because even if there is a chance of some unexpected movement in the price of the stock, you don't miss out on your profits or convert this winning trade into a losing one. No matter how good the conditions are now, you should never forget that changes in the market happen very quickly and swiftly. They don't give any warning. So, having a proper understanding of the risk you are taking is important so that you can take the necessary steps in case the market makes a move that is different from what you speculated.

Profits and Losses

The iron condor strategy is a limited profit strategy where your total profit from the trade is equal to the credit you receive initially while entering the trade. Maximum profit in this trade is calculated by subtracting the commissions you paid from this net credit. When the price of the underlying asset is present between the strike prices of the put and call you sold, then you achieve the situation of maximum profit. It is at this price that all the options you own expire worthlessly.

Now, let's talk about the risk involved. This is a strategy of limited risk like I told you at the beginning of this chapter. But you have to keep in mind that even this limited risk is quite more in amount than the maximum profit you'll attain here. The situation of maximum loss occurs when the price of the underlying asset decreases and it goes below the purchased put's lower strike price or goes above (or becomes equal to) the purchased call's higher strike price. If you fall in any of the above-mentioned situations, then maximum loss occurs, which is found out by calculating the difference between the strike price of the calls or puts and then subtracting the net credit you received while entering the trade from this value.

Iron Condor Example

Let us now move on to an example of the iron condor to make things even clearer and easier to understand. Suppose the stock of ABC company is trading at $45 in the month of June. Now, a particular trader who wants to construct the iron condor purchases at JUL 35 put for an amount of $50, sells a JUL 40 put for $100, sells another JUL 50 call for an amount of $100, and finally, purchases another JUL 55 call for $50. Upon performing all these transactions, the trader will be left with a net credit of $100. Like we discussed in the previous section, the maximum profit a trader can make from this strategy is limited to $100, which is his net credit at the time of entering this trade.

When the date of expiration approaches in July, let us assume that the stock is still trading at $45. In that case, all the options that you had will be expiring, and they will be deemed worthless. When that happens, you get to keep the credit you earned in the initial stage, that is, $100 as a profit after subtracting the commissions from it.

But if the stock, at the time of expiration, trades at $35 instead of $45, then the JUL 40 put that was sold will not expire, but the others will. The intrinsic value of this put is $500. If you want to exit this trade, then you will have to purchase the option back. Now, to calculate the total loss, you have to subtract the credit you received initially, which was $100. Upon calculation, the net loss comes to $400. The same situation would have arrived if the price of the underlying asset went up to $55.

Chapter 6

Bearish Strategies

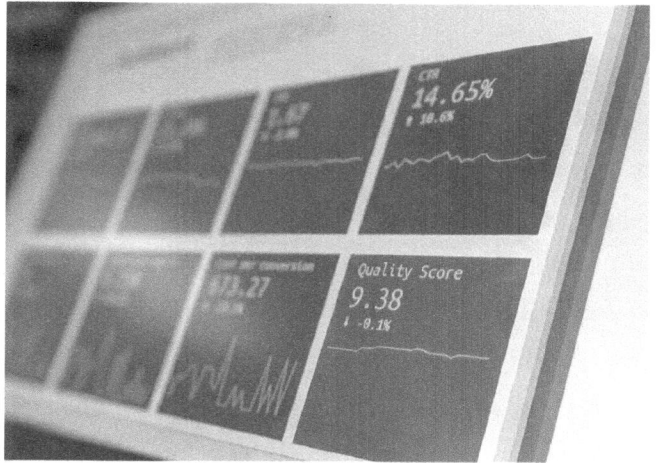

If you are expecting a fall in the value of the underlying asset, then your outlook of the market is bearish, and that is when you implement bearish strategies. In this chapter, we are going to study some of the most important bearish strategies in the world of options trading in greater detail.

Long Put

This is quite a basic strategy and perfect for any beginner. Here the trader will purchase put options because they are speculating that there will be a fall in the price of the underlying asset. The fall will be such that the price of the underlying asset will reduce below the strike price, and this has to happen before the date of expiration.

Now let's see whether short selling is more convenient than a long put or not. Well, to be honest, the long put is a much easier bet because, in order to short, you are not actually borrowing the stocks here. Moreover, you are being exposed to a limited risk in a long put as opposed to short selling where the risk is unlimited. But keep in mind that the lifespan of put options is always limited. If the price of the underlying asset does not manage to reduce and go below the strike price before the date of expiration of the option approaches, then the contract will expire, and the put option will become worthless.

The profit potential of a long put is substantial. This is because, theoretically speaking, when the contract reaches expiration, the price of the underlying asset can even drop to zero. So, you can calculate the maximum profit by subtracting the premium you paid for the option from the strike price of the long put.

The risk involved is limited, and it is capped to the premium you paid for the contract in addition to any commissions. The loss will remain capped to this value irrespective of how high the stock price rises.

Here's an example – let's say a stock ABC is trading at $100, and you think it will decrease in value. So, you purchase a put option at $2 with a strike price of $90. Now, if your prediction is correct and the price of the underlying asset reduces to $85, then you make $5, but you have already paid $2 for the options contract, so your net profit, in this case, will be $3.

Short Call

This is another common strategy for the investor with a bearish outlook of the market. If you sell the call and the option is assigned, then you will be under the obligation to sell the underlying asset at the strike price. Your aim should be for the call to reach the date of expiration and expire worthless. That is why it is advised that you should wait until the strike price of the option goes out-of-the-money by one standard deviation. You also want a reduction in the implied volatility so that there is a decrease in the price of the options. Remember that you will receive an even lower premium from this strategy if the strike price is higher. In fact, some traders do not prefer running this strategy on individual stocks but choose index options because if we see historical figures, you will notice that indexes are not as volatile as individual stocks. The volatility of the index as an entire entity reduces because the stock price fluctuations in the index component tend to cancel each other out.

Here, the maximum potential for profit by following this strategy is limited. The profit will be capped to the total premium you get after you sell the call. Also, you will keep losing more money if the price of the underlying asset keeps rising above the strike price.

Theoretically, the risk associated with carrying out this strategy is unlimited. You keep losing money with the rise in the price of the underlying asset, and the price can actually rise as much as it wants as so the risk becomes unlimited. So, if you indeed decide to carry on with this strategy, make sure you have a stop loss in place, and you stick to it no matter what.

Here's an example – let us say that a stock ABC is trading at a price of $100, and you want to sell a call option with a strike price of $110. And by doing so, you collect a premium of $2. Now, if the price of the stock increases to $115, you will be under the obligation to purchase the stock at $115 and then give the underlying stock at $110 to the buyer. In this transaction, you lose $5, but if you adjust the $2 that you received in the beginning, your net loss stands at $3. On the other hand, if the price of the underlying asset never reaches $110 or keeps trading downwards, then as profit, you get to keep the premium of $2.

Put Ratio Strategy

This basically falls under the category of neutral strategies, and in order to build this strategy, you will have to purchase a certain number of put options and then sell put options in greater numbers of the same underlying asset with different strike prices but the same date of expiration. If you think that in the near term, the underlying asset is going to face some volatility, then this strategy is perfect for you. For a 2:1 put ration spread construction, by purchasing a certain number of put options at a strike price that is higher and then selling double the number of put options at a strike price that is lower.

The profit potential in this strategy is limited, and you can find out the maximum profit made by following this strategy by subtracting the strike price of the short put from the strike price of the long put and then adding the net premium received to this value. You should also subtract any commissions that you paid. The situation of maximum profit will arise when at the date of expiration, the price of the underlying asset is equal to the strike of the short put.

The downside risk of the strategy is unlimited, but there is almost no or very little upside risk associated with this strategy.

Bear Call Strategy

There are two transactions involved in constructing a bear call spread strategy. You first sell an at-the-money call option, and at the same time, you purchase an out-of-the-money call option, and both of these options should have the same date of expiration and the same underlying assets. The main motive behind implementing this strategy is that you can make some good profits with limited risk exposure.

The maximum profit potential of this strategy is limited to the net credit you receive in the beginning. But to achieve this situation of maximum profit, both the option contracts need to expire worthless so that you are not left with any liability. That is why it is advised that you sell contracts that are at-the-money so that even if the price of the underlying asset remains the same or does not fall in price, you can still make money from it.

You will be facing a loss if your prediction of a bearish outlook goes wrong and there is an increase in the price of the underlying asset. At the time of expiration, if the contracts are in-the-money, then they can either be assigned, or you will be under the liability to buy them back and incur a loss. But the loss potential is limited, and the maximum loss can be calculated by finding the difference between the strike prices of the contracts you purchased and sold and then multiply it with the number of contracts written.

The flexibility of this strategy is its main advantage. If the underlying asset's price decreases, then you make a greater profit, but even if the price remains stable, you can make a profit then too. The second advantage is the fact that the loss is capped and so there are no chances of unlimited risk exposure. I will agree that compared to the other strategies, this one is a bit complicated, but if you are able to master it, it will be worth your while.

Bear Put Strategy

Just like the bear call strategy, this one also requires you to make two transactions. You have to purchase one at-the-money put and sell one out-of-the-money put, and both contracts should have the same date of expiration and have the same underlying asset.

The main aim of this strategy is to make a gain from the underlying security's price decrease. But there is another factor that can help you make a profit, and that is time decay because even if there is not a considerable drop in the underlying asset's price, the value will eventually decrease due to time decay.

The situation of maximum profit will arrive when the underlying asset's price falls to the level to become equal to the contracts' strike price at which they were sold. At this point, you will have no obligations in relation to the contracts you sold, and as for the contracts you bought, you will profit from their increase in value. But in case there is a fall in the underlying asset's price, even more, then you will start losing money on the contracts you sold. However, the net effect will be zero because there will be an increase in value in the puts you have purchased.

If there is a rise in the underlying security's price, then you will be losing money. You will also lose money if the price doesn't move at all or doesn't go as low as you need it to. But your loss is capped to the upfront investment you had to make in order to build this strategy.

Bear Put Ladder Spread

You have seen the bear put spread in the previous section, and now, this strategy is kind of an extension of the bear put spread. But you have to very precise with your speculation of downward movement in price. If the price goes down way more than you expected, then you are in for huge losses.

In order to construct the bear put ladder spread, you can initiate it in the following manner – purchase one at-the-money put, sell one out-of-the-money put, and sell one far-out-of-the-money put. All of these contracts should have the same date of expiration and be based on the same underlying asset.

The profit potential for this strategy is limited. You will arrive at the situation of maximum profit when the underlying asset's price will decrease and be at a level that is somewhere at a point that is present between the two put options' strike prices. In case the underlying security's price falls beyond the lowest strike price, then there will be a decrease in your profits, and if the decrease is too much, then you will ultimately incur a loss. If the underlying asset's price increases or does not undergo any such price change, then the initial investment you made to enter this trade will be lost.

This strategy should be carried out only when you are confident enough that there will be a fall in the underlying asset's price, but the decrease will not be too much to cause you a loss. Thus, the complexity of this strategy makes this one unfit for beginners.

Chapter 7

The Option Trader's Mindset – 10 Traits That Should be Present

As far as the overall financial market is concerned, options are considered to be quite versatile. You can increase your returns by leveraging your position, and this is possible because of the flexibility of options. These characteristics of options also make them suitable for hedging, and thus, they are an important tool of risk management. You can make a profit with them no matter what the condition of the market is. But even if it has countless benefits, options trading also has a substantial amount of risk, and the very nature of options trading is based on speculation. So, it is not everyone's cup of tea. If you want to be a successful options trader, there are some traits that you should definitely possess. In this chapter, we are going to discuss ten such traits that make a successful options trader and helps them hone their mindset.

Manage Risk Successfully

You already know that there is a high amount of risk associated with trading options, and thus, any trader who is thinking to step into this particular world must be an efficient risk manager. There are endless methods to do so. We are going to cover this topic in detail in Chapter 9 but here, I am going to give you a brief idea of what risk management looks like in options trading.

You all have heard of diversification, right? When it comes to the share market, we are repeatedly advised not to keep all the eggs in the same basket. The same applies to options. You can diversify your options in different ways, all of which will be discussed in detail later. Another important way in which you should manage your risk is optimal position sizing. The total trading capital that you are putting in options trading should not constitute a huge portion of your portfolio. In general, as a rule of thumb, your options trading capital should only be about 5% of your portfolio, so even if things go wrong, you don't lose everything. The same rule applies to individual trades as well.

Lastly, if you want to be an efficient trader, you need to be an expert in managing your money. That is why money management and risk management often go hand in hand.

Don't Make Mistake With Numbers

In options trading, there will be a lot of numbers involved, and you cannot afford to make mistakes with them. If you dive into technical analysis, which is crucial for planning your strategies, you will get even more numbers, and then there are the Greeks. You need to have proper knowledge of all of this. In short, your foundation of knowledge should be solid.

For every trade that you do, you will have to figure out certain technical indicators, what your maximum profit can be, what your maximum loss can be, and what is the breakeven point. And everything you do is all about numbers, and if you are bad with numbers, trading can be a nightmare for you.

Practice Discipline

No expensive software can gift you discipline. It has to be learned and inculcated by you. No matter how many seminars you attend or how many books you read, discipline is something that you can't buy with money. Self-control is a very important trait required in traders who come into options trading.

If you want to make profits consistently, trading discipline is essential. If you build a trading plan and then abandon it due to the lack of discipline, what good is the plan anyway? Traders who lack the sense of discipline make haphazard decisions and enter trades on a whim. This only leads to losses. Sometimes, there might be some unjustified reward that would make you feel that you don't need a trading plan to be successful. But this kind of thinking is going to be your downfall. Just because you got a reward once doesn't mean you will make the same profit again without the trading plan.

When you test your trading strategies over and over again and then use them, you are a more experienced trader than someone who does things randomly. But before you do anything, you have to hone your skills. A very big part of building this discipline is consistency. Don't let those random unjustified wins interfere with your mind or make you give up on discipline. Because without discipline, you will not be able to fetch profits in the long run.

Don't Rush

Successful traders are successful because they are patient with their trades. First of all, when you are just a beginner, the learning curve is going to be very steep. That is the first place where your virtue of patience will be put to the test. Secondly, when you are waiting for your trade to bring home profits, you have to wait for the perfect moment before you can close your position. That requires patience, too, and many newbies who don't have that make sudden decisions and ruin a trade that had the potential to be successful.

People in today's world have this craving for instant gratification that leads them to abandon patience. But with this attitude for instant gratification, you are never going to achieve anything good in life. Everything good needs patience and time. But as a beginner, if you are wondering how to be patient in trading, here are some steps that you can follow –

- Firstly, you have to be crystal clear on your 'why.' Why did you come into options trading in the first place? It is often easier to be patient and wait for results when your reason for coming into this field is strong enough to put you through all the hurdles that come your way. Some people say that they love to engage in options trading because they love the excitement associated with it. However, that is not a proper reason. If excitement is all you want, you are better off at a casino. But if your reasons are something like this – you want to leave your 9 to 5 job someday and become financially independent, or you want to support your family and give them a good life, or you want to build your dream house, or any other such dream then it comes easier to stick to that goal with patience until you master options trading.

- Secondly, never put all your focus on the money. People who only think about money are the ones who act out in very irrational ways because they engage in a fight or flight response. Your trades should be thought of individually. They should never be linked to the money in them. If you are finding it difficult to do so, then you can keep the profit/loss values away from your eyes and focus solely on the charts. You should also try not to keep watching your profit or loss values every hour. It is your trading plan that needs most of your attention, and if you follow it diligently, you are going to excel.

- Thirdly, before you enter any trade, make sure you have prepared a checklist of all the things you should keep an eye on. Whenever you find the time, go through the list. This will help you cover all your bases. Sometimes, when you are worrying too much, you might forget some important points that would lead to losses after entering the trade. But having a checklist at hand will prevent anything like that from happening.

- Make sure you get enough sleep; otherwise, your nerves will keep you on edge at all times, and you will find it even more difficult to be patient.

- Another effective thing to try in order to increase your ability to be patient is meditation. It works for a lot of people. Moreover, meditating will help you keep your focus on the here and now, and you will be less anxious. You no longer will take unnecessary stress about how much you might lose from a trade. When you are less stressed, you will be able to put your focus in the right place and remain alert so that whenever you see an opportunity to take your profits, you can exit the trade.

Figure Out Your Trading Style

Every successful trader has their own trading style, and you need to develop yours as well. When you are just a beginner, and you have just entered the options market, you will feel like you have to make so many decisions at once, and all of this will leave you confused, and you might even feel lost.

But once your trading style is figured out, many things will fall in place. Here are some questions that you should ask yourself because they will help you pinpoint what your trading style is.

- **What kind of market analysis are you going to employ?** Like you know, there are two types of market analysis – fundamental and technical. Even though for options, it is a technical analysis that serves to be more fruitful because options are financial instruments for the short-term, there are certain options that last for a long time, and they are known as LEAPS. For LEAPS, you can use fundamental analysis. So, figuring out which type of analysis you want to perform or are comfortable with will also help you find out which type of trading style you want to engage in.

- **Which securities do you want to trade in?** The underlying asset or security of an options contract can be anything. It can be something basic like stocks, or it can also be forex. It is entirely your own risk appetite or knowledge about that security that will help you make this decision. But every type of security has its own set of characteristics – some are more versatile than others, while some have a steep learning curve. Keeping all of these things in mind, you should make your decision.

- **What strategies do you want to use?** In this book, we have already covered many strategies that are commonly used in options trading. Every trader has their own preference of strategies when they are analyzing a trade. Some use moving averages, while others depend on stochastics. But in general, you should never be overburdening yourself with too many indicators at the same time; otherwise, it will become overwhelming and not be helpful at all. However, you should also try not to deviate too much from the mainstream. Moreover, there are certain technical indicators and strategies that are more suitable for beginners compared to others, and so, you should also keep this in mind while making your choice.

- **What time frame do you have in mind?** Even though options are traded mostly in the short-term, but they can be of varied time frames. It is entirely your call as to how long do you want to keep your money invested in an option. Every type of time frame in options trading has its own advantages and drawbacks, and they also affect people in a different way. Some people like to realize their gains or losses quickly, while others prefer playing it out for a long time. Whatever it is that you want, you need to decide on it first, and you will automatically know what your trading style is.

Understand the News

When you are in the world of trading, you have to keep up with all the latest events that can affect your trade. But does everything you see on the television hold equal importance? The answer is no, but many people fail to understand that. Some of it is pure hype, while the other half is what you actually need. Sometimes beginners often think that if they rely on the promising news they see on TV and put their money on a certain option, they may or may not get the desired results. But they will surely miss out on other important and possibly bigger trends in the market because they couldn't see anything outside of that news.

You should avoid any kneejerk reactions because you can be a successful trader only when you give a thought to each and every step and make rational decisions keeping in mind the objectives of your trade and your risk tolerance. No matter what you see on the news, never take your eye off the bigger picture. So, as much as it is important for you to pick up on important news, it is equally important for you to understand which news you should ignore.

Always Be Eager to Learn More

When you step into the world of options trading, I won't lie – it can be intimidating. The overall concept is not hard to understand, but in order to make consistent profits, you need to be aware of the subtle nuances and the several intricacies that come in between, and it is these intricacies that have a steep learning curve. Just because you lost a few trades doesn't mean you should give up. Every trader who is successful today has lost trades and still loses them. Losing is a part of winning – they come hand in hand. But what is important is that your profits should be more than enough to cover those losses and still be in excess.

Moreover, there is no one set path for everyone in trading. Everyone goes about it differently depending on the style that suits them the best. So, if you want to become successful at it one day, you need to do a lot of research and learn. You will have to accept that the learning curve of options trading is steep, and you are ready to learn despite that. If you are not sure where to start or what to do, here are some tips for you –

- **It's always best to take the help of a mentor.** If you have a knowledgeable person in your corner who can teach you the ins and outs of options trading from their own experience, there is nothing better than that. It would even be more useful and interesting for you to learn from someone who has himself faced everything that you are facing. When you are facing a tough situation in a trade, and you don't know what to do, it is a life savior to have a mentor to whom you can look up for a solution rather than gamble all your money away in a hasty decision. With the help of a mentor, it becomes easier for you to get off on the right foot with options. Your mentor has probably made the same mistakes that you are making or thinking of making, and so he can guide you through all your fears and apprehensions so that you don't fall into the same trap as they did.

- **Don't wander aimlessly.** The second most important thing to do is knowing what you are doing. Some people don't give much thought to things and simply let inertia carry them off to wherever it is taking them. But when you know all the reasons why something is happening or why you are doing what you are doing, it keeps you one step ahead of all those people who don't bother knowing such stuff. Moreover, you can make far more informed decisions during a trade. Never follow anything blindly. Do your own research, and success will keep coming in naturally.

Keep in mind that the condition of the market today might not be the same tomorrow. The very nature of markets is that they keep changing constantly, and if you want to be successful, you need to keep up with these changes. You need to keep checking whether your current trading strategies still apply in the changed market conditions or not; otherwise, you might miss out on some profitable opportunities in the market.

Be Flexible

Like I mentioned earlier, the market is going to throw a lot of curveballs at you, and you need to be able to handle them all. And for doing that, you need to be more flexible. Change, losses, and uncertainty are things that you will be facing from time to time, and it is your flexible nature that will help you get through all of this. But what does it mean to be flexible in trading? It means that you are not stringent in your way, and you understand when your current strategies need change. When a trader is able to do this, they can take up any challenge with a smile.

A flexible trader will never allow any particular to affect them to such an extent that they get bent out of shape. They don't spend too long procrastinating or ruminating over their strategies. They know what they want, and they get it. They always do their background research and homework so that when they need to act fast, they have all the information they need handy. Their trading plan is sensible and has room to breathe, and when they notice any probable opportunities cropping up, they don't doubt themselves. They snatch the opportunity. When they lose a trade, they don't feel self-reproach, and neither do they start bragging about every other win. They keep to themselves about such things and treat trading like the business it is. When they win, they know better than to give in to pride. They simply collect their profits at the right time and move on to the next trade. They know that even though they are winning one trade after the other, they might lose a trade or two in between. But they aim at making their wins so huge that a few losses don't leave a dent in their portfolio. They are always ready to adapt to changes, and most importantly, they are prepared to come out of their comfort zone.

Some people think that being flexible is about the condition you are in or the type of trade you are doing. But it's not that – being flexible is more about how you are as a person.

Always Have a Trading Plan

Every trader must have a trading plan. A trading plan is what will tell you how you should go about a trade. It will also make your objectives clearer and make you aware of the risks involved. You also have a clear idea of when you should trade and when you should walk away from a trade. In fact, you should not even risk your capital in the first place if you do not have your trading plan ready. In short, it is like a roadmap that you need to follow. If you are building a trading plan, these are some things that you should keep in mind –

- Every trading plan should have the trader's goals clearly mentioned. Your risk-reward ratios should be realistic and not something that is next to impossible to achieve. You should try setting goals on a weekly and monthly basis and then make a final annual goals section to review how your year went. You can set these goals as a percentage of your total portfolio or in dollars, but the most important thing is that you should reassess these goals from time to time.

- The next most important thing that every trading plan should have is the risk level you are willing to take. You should clearly mention the amount of risk you can afford to expose yourself to in each trade. This number usually varies from person to person, depending on their portfolio. Suppose you set your risk to 2% of your portfolio, and if you already have this much amount on that day, then you need to get out of the trade and cut off your losses any further. There's always going to be another day when you can fight, but today, you need to call it an end.

- When you make the trading plan, perform your homework. You need to do what is happening around the world and whether there are any major economic changes happening. You can decide the mood of the market with the help of index futures. You should also keep track of important dates, for example, when the earnings report of a particular company is coming out when some important news is going to be released, and so on. Experts never gamble with their money in trading – they make informed decisions.

- You should also set alerts to keep you notified about entry and exit signals.

- You should have a set of entry and exit rules. But first, work on your exits because they are far more crucial than your entries. And then figure out some effective entry points and strategies.

Apart from the trading plan itself, you should also plan each trade that you are going to make. Here is a step-by-step layout of how you should proceed –

- **Make the prediction** – The first step is to make a prediction or speculation to find an opportunity for your trade. You need to figure out how you can use this opportunity to your advantage and get some returns. In options trading, you already have the upper hand when it comes to making the prediction. No matter what your outlook of the market is, there is always a way in which you can strategize on it and make profits. Once your confident with your speculation, it's time to strategize.

- **Decide your targets** – I'll agree that you don't necessarily have to set targets for every trade you make, but this will keep you ahead. The main idea behind this is to reasonably set a target for how much profit you want to make from this particular trade. Another way in which you can set targets is by specifying the amount of time within which you want to make a certain amount of money. This will also ensure that you are not spending too much time tied up in a single trade.

- **Build your strategy** – Now comes the most important part of a trade – strategy. There are endless ways in which you can do this for a particular asset. But the main thing to understand here is that you will make a profit on your trade if you figure out what combination of strategies is right for you at a given time. While you are strategizing, there is something else that should be kept in mind as well – and that is – risk management. Your strategies should be well thought out and should not be exposing you to unlimited risk. In fact, your strategies should be minimizing the risk involved and maximizing the profit you get.

- **Set a position size** – After you have decided on your strategy for the trade, you will have to decide how much capital you are going to set aside for it, also known as the position size. If you want to effectively control your budget, then position sizing is a very important lesson. Even if you are highly confident about a trade, you should never be putting a lot of money into it. Always stick to your position size. Remember that position sizing is not about limiting the amount of money you are putting on the trade, but it is also about limiting the amount of money you are risking.

- **Decide your entry** – After this comes the part where you figure out your entry point into the trade. Use the various technical indicators so that you don't miss out on any red flags.

- **Plan your exit** – Even more important than your entry is your exit. If you don't have your exit planned before you enter a trade, you might be too late in collecting your profits, or you might go on a path of unlimited loss.

Maintain Records

Lastly, a very important trait of successful traders is that they record their trades in a journal. This might sound like a tedious task, but trust me, it is going to serve you well in the long run. It will require discipline and consistency, but it will also help you in several ways. Here are some ways in which maintaining a trading journal proves to be beneficial –

- **It will help you keep track of patterns and trends –** When you keep notes of your day-to-day trades, it helps you remember in the long-term which strategies worked for you in which scenario and which didn't. Keep note of the technical indicators or charts you used or whether there were any special events in the market and how they impacted your trade. For example, perhaps you took a signal too seriously, and it turned out to be a false one. When you write these things down in your journal, you will think twice before making the same mistakes again in the future.

- **Your trading technique will improve over time** – You will be able to understand your weaknesses and strengths in a better way when you note down every detail about your past trades. If you go through them later on, you will understand whether your decisions were right for you or did you make them from an emotional perspective. Thus, maintaining a trading journal helps you understand yourself as a trader, and thus, you will know which skills you have to improve on.

- **You can actively monitor your growth** – Your perspective will get messed up with your increasing time in trading. But when you write things down, you have greater clarity on your perspective. You can even look back on where you had started and where you are now. These things will give you an instant bout of motivation and push you to do better.

Thus, maintaining a trading journal will take you an inch closer to success. But most people don't journal the right way. You have to make an entry of your trades on a daily basis. If you keep them to be noted down at the weekend, you won't remember every detail. It's always better to document things when they are fresh in your mind.

So, these were the ten traits that every successful trader should have. Smart investment decisions and keeping a hold of your emotions are the two main things you need to put your focus on. Even if all this information feels intimidating now, don't lose hope – keep trying. With the right guidance and mindset, you will surely come out at the top and generate some good returns. Remember that options trading is a risky business, and you cannot go about it on a whim. You have to make well-informed decisions and practice patience to wait for the results of those decisions. But if you follow everything mentioned in this chapter, you will soon be trading options like a pro.

CHAPTER 8

How to Maximize Profits?

If you want to make substantial profits in options trading, you have to go about it in a calculated way with good strategies. When you have a proper strategy in place, it will help you reduce and manage your exposure to risk and also give you a clear idea of when to get in and get out of the trade. So, in this chapter, I am going to give you some tips or strategies that you should keep in mind if you want to maximize your profits in a trade.

What Are the Challenges That You Will Face in Options Trading?

Options trading is not the same as stock trading, and the sooner you understand, the better. There are a few challenges that you are going to face here, and before we move on to the profit-taking part of this chapter, I want you to be well-aware of these strategies because they are indeed some important constraints along the path –

- As you already know, stocks do not have any expiry, and you can hold on to them for any amount of time you want, but that is not the case with options. In an options contract, there is an expiration date. Thus, your trade has to be completed within that date of expiration, and so, if there are any viable opportunities that you miss, you might not get them back before expiration. So, it is important for you to be vigilant at all times and not miss out on any signals that can fetch you significant profit.

- In stocks, there are some strategies that are suitable for the long-term and are really good, for example, averaging down. But you cannot use them in the case of options because of the same reason – options have an expiration date and, thus, a limited lifespan.

- The capital requirements of a trade can be hugely impacted due to the margin requirements in options trading.

- If you find a price move that is favorable, you might not be able to bank on it so easily because the price of an option depends on numerous factors. For example, maybe the underlying asset of the option is showing favorable movements for you to bring home profits, but there are so many factors that can erode the profits in the short-term, like dividend payment, time decay, and volatility.

But there are ways in which you can maximize profits, and we are going to discuss them one by one.

Make Use of Trailing Stops

One of the most common and effective strategies of profit-taking in options trading is the use of trailing stops. Here, you set a particular percentage level (for example, 5%) for a particular target. Here is an example –

Let us assume that you purchase a total of 10 options contracts each of $80, and so you spend a total of $800. If your profit target is $100, let us say that your stop loss is at $70. Now, once the target of $100 profit is hit, there comes a trailing target, that is, $95, which is 5% lower. Now, if the trend keeps going in the same direction and now the price has moved to $120, then the trailing stop would also move up to $114. Now, if the trend suddenly changes and the price starts to move down, the option will be automatically sold at $114.

So, even when your gains are increasing, you keep getting the protection of a stop loss with the help of a trailing stop. This ensures that once the direction changes, you are out of the trade before you lose too much money. But something important to keep in mind here is that your stop loss level should never be too large, or it will be impossible to achieve, and at the same time, it should not be too small; otherwise, it will stand a chance to get triggered too easily.

Practice Booking Profit Partially at Targets

If you ask around some experienced traders, you will find a common habit in them – they book their profits partially once a certain set target has been reached. Let us say that the first target is $100, and if it is reached, they might be squaring off a 50% or 30% position. In the case of options trading, there are two main advantages of practicing this method, and they are as follows –

- You will be able to protect your trading capital to a great extent if you book your profits partially at targets. This is because in case the market reverses suddenly, you won't be losing all your capital. And in options trading, sudden market reversals are quite common. In the example that we used in the previous section when the target of $100 is reached, the trader can choose to sell 5 out of 10 contracts so that $500 worth of capital is retained with him.

- When the rest of the position is left open, the trader also has the opportunity to take full advantage of the future gains. When the target of $120 is hit, and the trader sells the rest of the contracts, he brings home a profit of $600, and thus, his total profit stands at $1100. You can do this division of profit-taking based on your preference. In the example, there was a 50-50 division, but you can also do a 60-40 division.

When to Take Profits in a Trade?

One of the most difficult things about options trading is exiting the market at the right time. It takes time to maneuver this. If you have made profits, it is also important that you don't gamble them away. Make wise decisions, and don't be greedy. Here are some tips that will come in handy –

- **When to hold them?** If you noticed any huge move either up or down, or if you are not too sure about the position you are holding and you are feeling uncomfortable, then are you sure about holding your position? Well, this can be figured out in a minute – ask yourself whether the components that drove you to this trade in the first place are still intact or not. If they are, then you can hold the trade. Let's say that you have invested in the put options after assessing the fundamentals, but even now, the position is not working in your favor yet. At the same time, the company is showing signs of weakness and is following a technical pattern that points in a downward direction. If you are ahead of the Wall Street is assessing the company, and if your fundamental assessment is still in place, then you should not leave your position just yet. But all of this might sound easier now. When it comes to acting on it, it takes a lot of nerves and experience to stick to the plan.

- **When to fold them?** If you have this question in your mind, then you again need to think back to the time you entered the trade and see whether your reason for entering the trade in the first place is still intact. Suppose you have purchased a put option of a not-so-sound company, but soon it becomes a target of acquisition, and their condition becomes better with increased earnings. Or, there is some major change in some other fundamental aspect, and whatever you speculated is so longer the same. In that case, you have to start taking steps to cut off your losses as much as you can.

- **When to walk away?** There are two situations where you should be walking away from a trade. The first is when you have accumulated profits. And the second situation is when you are nearing a condition of loss. Your ultimate aim should be to protect your portfolio. Many traders forget about their portfolios when they are trading. Remember that your trades are not floating in space – each and every one of them contributes to your portfolio.

When to run? Everyone has a different goal of profit when they enter a trade. Let us say that your goal is to double your investment. And if you hit that 100% mark on your trade, you need to get out as fast as possible and take your profits. Another reason to quickly run is when the market is about to change completely.

Chapter 9

Risk Management Techniques

Like I already told you at the beginning of this book, options were initially introduced as a hedging strategy. But when you are stepping into the world of options trading, there will be certain risk factors coming your way that you need to manage. You not only have to try and reduce your risk exposure as much as possible, but you also have to actively manage your capital. Whenever you are making any investment, risk should always be tried and kept at bay, but at the same time, you should also keep in mind that exposure to risks shouldn't be a problem in trading. This is because every successful trader must learn ways to effectively manage the risk. Also, never walk out of your zone of comfort when it comes to risk. If you are taking a certain level of risk, you should be comfortable taking it up in the first place. Never put yourself in a position where you are being exposed to an unlimited loss.

In this chapter, I am going to introduce you to some effective methods with the help of which you can manage your risk and minimize the chances of incurring a loss.

Determine Risk/Exposure Upfront

The first step is to obviously make a proper assessment of the risk involved, and this should be done upfront and not after you have entered the trade. As you all know, trading in options is all about buying and selling of puts and calls. You might have also heard of the term risk/reward ratio. In general situations, it is considered that the higher the risk you are willing to take, the higher will be your potential for profit. But all this said and done, many traders, especially beginners, fail to assess how much risk is suitable for them. Moreover, it is important for you to figure out how much risk your portfolio would be able to carry.

So, how are you going to find out this risk preference? For starters, I'd like to say that every trader is different, and so it's not that easy to follow any single model for determining risk. But there are two very crucial and fundamental things to keep in mind when you want to assess your risk, and they are as follows –

- **Time Horizon** – You obviously have a certain duration of time in your mind for which you want to keep your money invested. And if you haven't decided on the time horizon yet, then that is your first priority. Options are usually traded over a short span of time, but there are some options that last longer as well. However, as a general rule of thumb, when you are trading over a shorter span of time, the volatility is much more, and thus the risk of losing your investment is also high. But when you are choosing a longer horizon of time, the risk automatically reduces.

- **Bankroll** – The second factor to consider while assessing your risk tolerance is how much money you can afford to lose from this trade. In this way, you will be able to make realistic decisions. If you don't want to face any issues with liquidity or panic and sell off your investments, then trade only with the money that you know you can afford to lose.

Lastly, I will like to remind you that not every trader is created equal. Investors with a considerably high net worth often have a high-risk tolerance before they can afford to lose that much money. The important thing to keep in mind is that you should never make any decisions on a whim or based on what others are doing. Your situation is not the same as the other person, so your risk preference has to be assessed separately.

Set Optimal Stop Loss Level

In trading, stop loss is a very important risk management tool because it prevents you from falling into a pit of uncontrollable losses. We will discuss why an optimal stop loss level should be set, but first, you need to know what a stop loss is. A stop loss is a point upon reaching which your position is automatically closed to prevent any further losses beyond that point.

Here are some of the reasons why setting an optimal stop loss level is necessary –

- **Your capital is finite** – No one has an endless source of capital – not even the richest people on this planet. Your capital is always a finite entity. And if you are a small trader, then your capital is even more constricted to a certain amount. A very big trader might trade-in options with very high risk because their risk appetite is more, but even then, they will be setting a stop loss because their capital will come to an end if they incur repeated losses. As a trader, one of your primary goals is to protect your capital, and a stop loss will prevent such an erosion from happening. So, for every trade you make, ensure that you have your maximum loss capacity figured out.

- **You can churn your money faster** – This is another benefit of using stop losses. Options primarily belong to the short-term trading category, but even then, if you keep your money invested in a losing trade for a long time, it's not going to help you achieve anything. So, if you see that it is not going well for you in a trade, you need to come out of it and move on. You need to compensate for that bad trade. And when you have a stop loss, the money will be churned out quickly.

- **It takes a lot of effort to bounce back after a loss** – If we are talking about recovering from losses, then statistics show that it is not so easy to bounce back and actually takes a lot of effort. For example, if you have faced a 10% loss, then to achieve the status quo, you will need at least 11% profit. So if you don't want this to happen, use a stop loss.

But there's something else to consider here – applying stop losses is easier when it comes to stocks. In the case of options trading, the techniques are slightly different. Let us say that the implied volatility of an option you own suddenly exploded; in such a case, it is quite natural for the stop-loss to get triggered. So, you will be left out of a profit-making situation. Similar to the process of shorting stocks, if you are selling a call or a put option, a buy-stop order can be used. Your losses will be limited if the price of the stock is going above the price you marked as the stop loss because the options will then be purchased at the market price.

Diversify Your Portfolio

You must have heard of diversification as a risk management solution in several places. But did you know that it is used in options trading as well? Yes, and I am going to explain to you how you can do it. First, you need to understand the main aim behind diversification. When you spread your investment over different financial instruments, you don't have to worry about any single instrument suffering a loss because you have others to compensate for it.

But when it comes to options trading, there are four different ways with the help of which you can diversify your investment, and they are as follows –

Diversify by Position Size

This is probably the most widespread strategy of diversification in the field of options. Most experts will tell you that your options trading portion should be a very small percentage of your total investment portfolio. And apart from this, you should maintain the position size of individual trades as well. Each trade should not be more than, say 5%, of your entire portfolio of options trading.

Even if this seems easy and efficient in words, it is completely the opposite in reality, and following this method is going to create a lot of hassle for you. Here's why –

- Firstly, it requires lots of effort. You will have to identify about 20 trades or more, track them, and manage them so that, in total, they comprise 5% of your overall portfolio. And if you are a small trader, the total amount that these trades would make might not be worth all the hard work you are putting in.

- If you think you have diversified your portfolio by building option trades with, say, 20 different securities, all of which have the same date of expiration, then you need to rethink. Let us assume that you follow a bullish strategy on all of these, but in reality, the market goes in the completely opposite direction, and there is a decline of 5-10%. What do you think would be the result? Would it matter that you had chosen your options after thorough research?

- Lastly, this method of diversification is fruitful mostly for people who have a significant portfolio, and if you don't have that, this is going to turn out mostly inefficient for you. There would be the bid-ask penalty and hefty commissions, all of which will start taking a toll on you. Your cost basis will become more efficient if you are able to bundle together a larger number of contracts under a single trade.

Diversify by Trading Strategy

Once I go into the details of this approach, I am sure that you will find it quite interesting. You might get a limited amount of protection from risk if you are mixing up your strategies and not sticking to just one.

Let us say you have already set up bullish trades on certain contracts, and for some others, you have used bearish strategies. In this case, even if there is a major uncanny market move that you were not anticipating, your entire portfolio won't be jeopardized. Just like this, another thing that you can do is set up complementary trades, meaning trades that will make profit from an increase in volatility and trades that will make a profit from a decrease in volatility.

And while we are talking about this, I would like to remind you that there are certain option trading strategies that following this method of diversification. For example, in iron condors, you are relying on the fact that on the upside, the stock won't go above a certain price, and on the downside, the stock won't go below a certain price before the date of expiration approaches. Both the legs of such trade have to be collateralized, and you can safely say that you are covered. And the maximum loss that you can face in extreme situations is 50%, better than your entire portfolio, right?

Diversify by Strike Price

Compared to the other two methods of diversification mentioned above, diversification by strike price has a little bit more promise. When you make small adjustments to the strike prices, you will see that your overall risk has been slightly reduced, but how?

Well, irrespective of the trade that you have set up or the strategy that you have employed, your chosen strike prices somewhat act as a knob that could adjust the position of your portfolio on the risk-reward scale.

To make this concept easier to understand, consider the example of how a covered call is built –

- Let us assume that you have purchased a stock whose price is $50 and then, you go on and write a covered call with a strike price of $55. With a 10% move towards the upside, you make a profit and also gain a little bit from the premium itself.

The premium you paid is your downside protection (which I agree is not much).

- On the contrary, if we consider that you have set up your trade at $47.50, that is, a lower strike price, then the premium you receive is way more. At the same time, on the upside, you are not profiting from any move, but you should also keep in mind that because of this strategy, the stock has to fall a lot in order for you to incur a loss.

Diversify by Time

If you ask me, I'd say this form of diversification is one of my favorites. There are several factors that affect the market, and if all the trades that you have made have the same date of expiration, then your profit-taking might be impacted by certain short-term factors. Always remember that the conditions of the market are never stagnant. If the market is behaving in a particular way today, there's no promise of it doing the same thing tomorrow, or three months from now, or later. This is a natural form of diversification, and if your trades are all expiring on the same day, that is, 30-days from now, you will lose out on this benefit.

So, as you see, there is no single way of performing diversification in options trading, and there is no right or wrong way as well. It all depends on the approach you prefer and are comfortable with and your trading style.

Keep Your Risk Consistent and Manage Your Emotions

There is a common tendency among beginner traders to increase their position size just because they say a few simultaneous wins. But you should never walk on this path until and unless you want your entire portfolio ruined. The risk levels you take should be kept consistent.

Winning two or three trades or even more in a row doesn't mean that all other trades are going to be the same. You should never make that assumption if you want to be a successful trader. Being confident is good, but being over-confident is going to be your downfall. When people become over-confident, they shut their eyes to everything else and become less risk-averse. Before you began trading, you had decided on position size, right? It is important for you to stick to that position size for the rest of your trading life.

It is true that trading can take a toll on your energy and drain you. So, it is important to take breaks; otherwise, you will be making all the wrong decisions. Remember that your brain is constantly dealing with both losing and winning. Thus, it's a rollercoaster ride for the brain. This might sound easy, but it is not so for your brain. And mastering your emotions is the first step to get it right.

One thing that helps is researching successful traders. Human beings have the tendency to follow suit. If you read the stories of some famous traders, you will see that all of them have lost numerous trades. But they never let their emotions take over their decisions. Your ultimate aim is to generate more money, but you also have to reduce and manage the risk that comes your way.

Secondly, keep in mind that losing money is completely fine. It happens to everyone. If you are in trading for the long-term, you cannot avoid losing money. No matter how much preparation you take for it, it is going to happen today or tomorrow. But losing money doesn't necessarily have to be a bad thing. Your goal should be to make larger profits compared to your losses so that you make progress. And lastly, just because you are doing well this month doesn't mean that you will be performing the same way in the next month as well. So, don't unnecessarily double your trades. Markets are usually highly volatile, and so if you are thinking about increasing your portion of the investment, you need to give it a lot of thought and consideration.

Maintain a Positive Risk-Reward Ratio

Controlling your exposure to risk is one of the main strategies to master if you want to be a successful options trader. You will often find profit/loss diagrams in options trading and other forms of trading as well, and these diagrams are known as risk graphs. So, for a single option position or spread, the profit you might gain or the loss you might incur is shown on this graph. You can find the current price of the underlying asset at the center of the graph. Now, as a trader, you should learn to use these graphs as they will benefit you in many ways.

Let us say that you have spent $100 in buying calls, and you speculated that sometime in the future, you are going to sell them at $300. But by doing this, you are also putting that entire $100 at risk in case the options expire worthlessly. If you manage to sell the calls at $300, then you make a profit of $200. Thus, your risk-to-reward ratio, in this case, would be $200 divided by $100, that is, 2:1.

There are expert traders who work out this ratio for every position they plan to enter. This helps them to make informed decisions. A minimum ratio of 4:1 is usually set by traders, and only then do they enter a position. Since options are quite volatile as financial instruments, it's important for you to control your risk exposure, and the risk-reward ratio will help you to a great extent.

Make the Best Use of Option Spreads

One of the crucial techniques of risk management in options trading is to use options spreads. We have covered the topic briefly in Chapter 2. When you combine multiple positions in a contract, all of which are of the same underlying asset, it creates an option spread.

When you are entering a position, the upfront costs involved in it can be reduced to a great extent with the help of option spreads. This also decreases the overall money you'd lose in case things don't go your way. Yes, along with the risk, the profit potential is reduced too, but you also have a lot less risk exposure. When you are entering a short position, there too spreads can come in quite handy.

In simpler terms, options spread work on the idea that you are relying on a combination of options contracts that will prove to be the most profitable.

Even though some people think that risk management is old-school, don't listen to them. You'd be a fool to ignore something as important as your risk exposure. Learning the techniques of risk management will help you thrive in the market for a longer time and fetch handsome profits. I hope this chapter has been useful in teaching you some strategies that you can use in your trading plan as well.

Conclusion

Thank you for reading *Options Trading Crash Course* until the very end. I really hope that you have been able to sort out all those things you were seeking the answers to and that you have everything you need to fulfill your goals.

The next step is to start walking on this path. Now that you have a general idea of where to begin, make your first trade. Yes, you will make mistakes along the way, but don't let those mistakes intimidate you into quitting. A word of caution – just because you have to begin somewhere doesn't mean you will put your money in a trade and not understand what you are doing – that's the exact rookie mistake that is the downfall of most beginners. You need to make well-researched and informed decisions. So, before you begin, make sure you have covered your basics and understood how these strategies work.

Make small trades. Don't go for too big position sizes; otherwise, you will end up hurting your portfolio. And even if you face a loss, try improving your strategy or figure out what went wrong. But never double down on the next trade just to cover your loss. You never know how this next trade is going to go. If it doesn't go your way, it might blow up your entire account. Praying and hoping that things will go as you speculated them to be is not how trading works. Not every trade is going to be a winning trade, but you have to give your best in each one of them.

If you think that all this knowledge is being too much for you, focus on one thing at a time. And when you learn something, test out your strategy through paper trading. Remember that learning options trading is not anything alien. It's like learning anything else. You need patience and commitment and always be clear on your 'why.' This will ensure that even if you are having a bad day, you can remember your 'why' and feel motivated. It takes dedication to master the art of options trading. It is okay to be discouraged at times, but it's not okay to quit. And lastly, this is not a get-rich-quick scheme. It is a skill that requires brushing up, so consistency is the key.

I would also appreciate it if you can leave a review on Amazon if this book helped you in any way.

www.ingramcontent.com/pod-product-compliance
Lightning Source LLC
LaVergne TN
LVHW091554060526
838200LV00036B/834